Quit Smoking
in *4 Steps*

FRANCIS X. KAMIENSKI, PHD
PHARMACOLOGIST, TOXICOLOGIST

MINDSTIR MEDIA

Published by Mindstir Media, LLC
45 Lafayette Rd | Suite 181| North Hampton, NH 03862 | USA
1.800.767.0531 | www.mindstirmedia.com

Printed in the United States of America
ISBN-13: 979-8-9860614-1-2

INTRODUCTION

Let's face it. More often than not, stopping smoking is a difficult business, and quitting is seldom contemplated with pleasure. Logically, it could be argued that if quitting were easy, you would have done it by now and wouldn't need any help. If you're like most people, you wished that somehow—magically—you could be rid of the habit without going through a withdrawal period.

How many times have you considered and actually tried to quit without results? Perhaps several times. In some cases, you almost quit but couldn't close the deal. Well, help is on the way. The program I outline with stepwise procedures will help you to reach the ultimate goal—to quit smoking!

How do I know this program will work? It worked for me—and others. I smoked for 26 years. I was puffing away two packs a day before I quit. This program guided me through the processes, which made quitting a dream. To this day I have no desire or craving to touch or put another cigarette to my lips, nor have I had any withdrawal symptoms. This program and your dedication will help you to quit smoking permanently.

NOTE:

I have provided several charts in the Appendices to help you monitor your progress as the program proceeds. These charts will serve as reminders that you should adhere to the program and that the exercises are working.

HEALTH ASPECTS

We know smoking is not good for your health. Cigarettes contain nicotine, which is highly addictive. It causes cancer, heart disease, strokes, lung cancer, chronic obstructive pulmonary disease, emphysema, chronic bronchitis and shortness of breath. Smoking also increases risk for tuberculosis, certain eye disease and problems of the immune system. In summary, smoking is bad for your health.

FINANCIAL COSTS

Smoking is expensive. Costs for cigarettes have skyrocketed in the last several years and continue to increase. Bottom line—quitting smoking will fatten your savings in no time!

BREAKING A BAD HABIT

This program, designed to overcoming smoking, is basically a step-wise program to break a bad habit. It is tailored especially for die-hard smokers but will work for smokers in general. Even though this program has been expressly designed to make quitting as easy as possible, it might be tough going for a while. But life changes, and so do people. This may be your time to change.

RATIONALIZATIONS

Most smokers know the harm they are doing to themselves. To keep smoking, therefore, we resort to various psychological maneuvers, clever attempts to justify or block out the basic and unpleasant truth about smoking and health.

Rationalizations are the most common excuses to quitting. These excuses try to make something unreasonable seem reasonable. But no matter how you slice them, rationalizations are still baloney.

There is no way you can continue to smoke without these self-deceptions, though it is possible to block any awareness that you are doing so.

Let's examine some of the most frequently used rationalizations below—and there are many—and see how they work. A chart in Appendix 1 can be used to monitor your rationale(s). Mark all the items that might apply to you.

1. "I don't smoke enough to harm myself." If you smoke at all, you are harming yourself. The human body was not designed to have its insides polluted by smoke or toxins.

2. "Oh, what the hell...." or ... "If it's not one thing, it's another." People who use this rationale are pulling the wool over their eyes

by telling themselves that cigarettes are only an insignificant danger in an already dangerous world.

3. "Cigarettes relax me." In truth cigarettes are not capable of relaxing anyone—they have the opposite effect on your body processes. What actually relaxes you are the things you do while smoking.

4. "Cigarettes pep me up." Though nicotine is a stimulant, it only works temporarily. As you smoke, you receive less vital oxygen as you breathe. The membranes of the air sacs in your lungs get clogged with the by-products of smoking, and carbon monoxide and other harmful gases reduce your oxygen supply and you lose energy.

5. "I'll gain too much weight if I quit smoking." Studies have shown that the average weight gain for people who quit smoking is usually less than five pounds. An actual survey reported a figure of only 3 ½ pounds!

6. "I don't have the willpower" is not something you are born with. However, it is something you can alter, develop or be taught. If you think "I don't have any willpower," it is because you have been taught to believe it, and you are probably continuing to teach yourself this idea in ways you are not aware of...yet.

BOTTOM LINE:

Once you stop rationalizing, you are closer to quitting smoking.

MATERIALS/SUPPLIES

The only materials needed in this program to quit smoking are:

- ballpoint pen
- rubber bands
- cloves
- newspaper

If you have these materials, you are on your way to quitting smoking. Also, if you truly want to stop smoking, you will cooperate with an open mind and give the program the proper attitude and determination to help it work for you.

Attitude is most important in making this program work for you. If you say "I'm going to try to quit" rather than "I'm going to quit," you probably won't be successful. The positive mind set is, of course, "I'm going to quit."

PRELIMINARY READING

Be aware this program will require willpower and will guide you step by step how to be successful. I suggest that before starting this program you read through the materials to understand what will be required. Your first impression after perusing the program is that it might be intimidating or overwhelming—well, it is not. By dismantling any project, including this program, into small easy steps and following them religiously makes the end goal doable and tangible with a minimum of stress. This same principle applies to quitting smoking.

STEP 1 (WEEK ONE)

Preparatory Reading

Let's get started. During the first preparatory week you will lay the groundwork for the changes that will follow. It is crucial to build the best foundation you can by reflecting on what you've read, considering the ramifications, rereading the material and, of course, by doing the exercises diligently.

STARTING THE EXERCISES

Remember these things before you start the exercises:

1. All work requires energy. You must expect to have some resistance or face some hard spots.

2. All changes take time and practice. Be patient with yourself, kind to yourself and considerate to yourself, because your "self"

is at work. Don't punish yourself for mistakes—they are inevitable. Forgive yourself and learn from your mistakes.

PITFALLS

Don't begin rationalizing. You're likely to say: "Well, I really don't have to do these particular exercises because…"

1. He's only using this program as an example—he doesn't expect me to do it.

2. This doesn't apply to me because my situation is different.

3. I don't really have to do it the way he says—I'll do it my way (most often in a way that won't work as well or will work toward the wrong goals).

Do all exercise assignments as precisely and faithfully as possible.

BREATHING AND IMAGING

Each day for the first week spend at least two (the more the better) five-minute periods as follows:

- Get to a quiet spot alone, sit down, close your eyes, take a few long deep breaths, and then picture yourself throwing away your last package of cigarettes into a blazing fire. In my case, my family built a small fire on our patio and ignited the cigarette pile with all of us cheering. That was a truly memorable occasion embedded in my memory. As you imagine yourself doing this, take another long, deep breath and relax. Follow this program and you will be the one igniting the cigarette pile.

- If you are not able to get a clear image at first, keep practicing. It will get better eventually. It may take a week or more to be perfect. Bring this image to your mind several times during each five-minute meditation period. Keep a reminder with you to practice or enter the times on the enclosed chart (Appendix 2) that you practice each day. Do it as precisely as described.

TRACKING CIGARETTE CONSUMPTION

*EACH DAY BEFORE YOU START OUT, OR JUST BEFORE RETIRING THE NIGHT BEFORE, MARK AN "X" ON ONE CIGARETTE IN YOUR PACK (NO MATTER WHETHER THE PACK IS NEW OR USED), SO YOU WILL NOT MISS IT. PUT THIS CIGARETTE BACK IN RANDOM ORDER. IF YOU SMOKE MORE THAN ONE PACK A DAY, DO THIS WITH ONE CIGARETTE IN EACH PACK AS SOON AS YOU OPEN IT.

DIRECTIONS FOR MARKING "THE LAST" CIGARETTE

1. Smoke as many cigarettes as you like this week. Don't try to stop prematurely. Examine each cigarette before you light it. If it has an "X" on it, crumple it up and throw it away. After each "X" cigarette, wait at least one hour before you smoke another cigarette.

2. Examine your rationalizations about stopping smoking, if and when they occur during the week, and analyze them to uncover their faulty premises. It will help if you write them down. The chart in Appendix 1 will assist you out in keeping tract.

3. Weigh yourself daily and record it (Appendix 3). Keep a list of the weights for 30 days or so. After you weigh yourself each day, record your weight next to the date in the provided chart.

4. Gradually increase the amount of exercise you do each day. It's best to emphasize one form of exercise. It can be anything—jumping rope, jogging, or walking more vigorously—and for greater distances than usual. Record the daily duration time each day of the exercises (s) you engage in (Appendix 4).

   Do not tire yourself by doing too much exercise too soon. The increase in exercise should be controlled so that it is not very unpleasant. If it is not a comfortable increase for you, it may be a sign that you are taking on a bit more than you should.

5. Keep a written tally of the number of cigarettes you smoke each day this week using the chart in Appendix 5. You will need to use the average of this week's daily cigarette consumption as a baseline to demonstrate your progress in future weeks.

There is evidence, incidentally, that in merely keeping a record of a habit you are already beginning to reduce its intensity and frequency. You may discover yourself smoking less before you expected to do so.

Be sure to read "Pitfalls" and the "Exercises" sections once each day.

Most people who start programs such as this are impatient and want to stop smoking at once. Hang on. Try not to stop until you reach the "QUITTING DAY"—THE BIG DAY!

So there, you have exposed yourself to your first step (week 1) of the program. If you have diligently followed the exercises, you have taken a huge step and are well on your way to quitting.

Wait a full week before you begin the next step and...practice what you learned

STEP 2 (WEEK TWO)

The Robot Smoker

This is the second of four steps (weeks) outlining how to arrest the "Robot Smoker" described below. Please note that within each smoker, an insistent Robot Smoker demands cigarettes, even while our rational minds and coughing bodies protest.

COUNTING CIGARETTES

Now that you counted the cigarettes you smoked each day for a week, add the daily figures, divide by seven and get a daily average. Then divide this number by three and subtract this number from the daily average to get the number of cigarettes you will smoke each day this week: one-third fewer cigarettes each day than you did last week (refer to chart in Appendix 5). The goal here is to smoke one-third the number of cigarettes each previous week.

THE HEALTH BANK AKA THE PIGGY BANK

For each cigarette you eliminate, save a certain sum of money in a separate place—as much as you can afford without taxing your budget. Label these savings as your personal "Cigarette Piggy Bank." You'll be surprised by the amount of money you have saved after the program is completed.

ANTICIGARETTE BRAND

Select an "anticigarette brand," one that you are least likely to enjoy. Cutting down on your own brand is harder than cutting down on one you do not like. If you smoke filters, buy non-filters, or vice versa: if you smoke menthol, buy non-menthol, and if you like a high tar brand, buy a "low tar brand" cigarette, etc.

People refer to the cigarettes they smoke as "my brand." How did you come to select the "my brand" of cigarettes you smoke? What influenced your choice? No matter what reason you give, it is likely to be a rationalization. "Your" brand of cigarettes is actually not "your" brand at all. The "you" or the "self," the most basic, most essential part of who you are, is always and forever a nonsmoker.

Smoking does not come easily or naturally to us. The pressure to do so must be so great and very persistent. In my case, starting to smoke was pure peer pressure. Initially, I turned down offers to smoke. But after considerable persistence, I caved and was prompted to smoke my first cigarette. I thought I was going to expire. I'm sure you can recollect why and how you had your first cigarette. The consequences of these events are addressed further in this program.

As you became dominated by the smoking addiction, you smoked more automatically. When you become hooked, you act as if you were controlled by an outside force, like a robot. This addicted scenario is called the "Robot Smoker." But a healthy part of you is ready to be revived, ready to restore health and reason.

Given proper support and encouragement, this life-affirming principle within each of us called the "self" can defeat the destructive, life-denying Robot Smoker.

The rejection of the Robot Smoker is the major operating principle of this program, and this is what you must make happen: you must increase your human capacity to choose freedom over the bondage of addiction, health over disease, the "self" over the Robot Smoker.

After smoking for many years (in my case 26 years), the habit inevitability becomes linked to certain recurring events, many of them pleasurable, like smoking with coffee, smoking after a meal, smoking while watching TV, smoking before going to bed, smoking after sex (not before), smoking while having a drink, and so forth.

With these and other linkages you are behaving like a conditioned animal in a laboratory, very much like Pavlov's dog. This automatic and unconscious process that links a cigarette with an activity is called a conditional reflex, and each time you repeat it, it becomes stronger. A vicious cycle is consequently set up!

Obviously, many of these associations were modeled after how others use smoking, like relatives, friends, strangers, celebrities and movie stars. Still other linkages may have been of your design. The more of these associations or linkages you have and the more often they occur, the more cigarettes you smoke.

In the early fifties, many movie stars and celebrities brandished cigarettes. It was the cool thing to do. Numerous ads extolled the virtue of cigarettes with catchy slogans such as, "I'd Walk a Mile for a Camel," "Lucky Strike Means Fine Tobacco" or "Call For Phillip Morris." Even sponsors of newscasters—such as John Cameron Swayzee—extolled the use of tobacco (in this case Camel cigarettes).

CONDITIONED REFLEXES

Another exercise is to write down a list of your personal conditioned reflexes (refer to Appendix 6). When do you smoke or when do you want to smoke? Select one as the first project of this week's phase of the program. It will be the one situation where you will deliberately refrain from smoking.

SMOKING MYTH

We now need to explore and explode a myth about stopping smoking. There is a commonly held belief that when a person gives up a habit like smoking, a new bad habit always and automatically "pops up" to take its place. It's called symptom substitution.

There is no scientific reason to support this notion. If you do experience an increase in any other troublesome behavior while quitting smoking, deal with it separately.

Consider that any such pattern has been there all along, but has been hidden by a smoke screen—your smoking habit.

TO BREAK THE SMOKING HABIT—INDEED, TO BREAK ANY HABIT— YOU MUST "RELOCATE" THE SOURCE OF ITS CONTROL FROM THE UNCONSCIOUSNESS TO THE CONSCIOUS MIND (THIS IS FUN- DAMENTALLY WHAT IS MEANT BY THE RATHER OVERWORKED TERM "CONSCIOUSNESS RAISING)."

You will need to raise your level of awareness about the way your "knee jerks," or automatic responses operate. In effect, you must banish the Robot Smoker from its comfortable home within you.

To do this, we will put you through a little ritual. Wrap your cigarettes with a piece of newspaper held on by a rubber band so a cigarette cannot be removed without taking off the band and unwrapping the paper. This will help you raise your awareness and "de-robotize" yourself, the next step in gaining ownership of your "self."

If you are asked by anyone why you have your cigarettes wrapped, say something like, "It's part of a program that I'm engaged in to stop smoking."

From this week on, wait five minutes from when you actually take a cigarette from the pack. At first this may seem to be a long time, but after smoking a few times you will probably hardly notice the minutes passing.

In addition, start counting slowly from one through five (about five seconds) between drags. Do this at random, whenever you think of it, at least two or three times with each cigarette.

What have you told yourself so far about your smoking habit? What are your personal myths about smoking? When was the last time you examined them? These questions are meant to be taken seriously. Therefore, do not read on any further until you have actually reflected on and answered these questions.

The cigarette-smoking habit rests upon ideas that have usually been unexamined, notions that are actually quite different from the way they appear to be on the surface.

SUMMARY OF EXERCISES OF WEEK TWO

1. Visualize at least once a day, for about five minutes, the image of throwing your last package of cigarettes in a fire.

2. Calculate the number of cigarettes you smoked per day last week and, as you begin each day this week, take with you exactly two-thirds of that average and no more (Appendix 5).

3. At the beginning of each day, wrap your pack of cigarettes or cigarette case in a sheet of newspaper fastened with a rubber band. Replace the rubber band and the paper after each cigarette.

4. Save money in a "health bank" for each cigarette less than your average—as much as you can comfortably afford.

5. Slightly increase the amount of exercise you do this week from last week. The increase should be definite but gradual, not exhausting.

6. Change to an "anticigarette," a brand that is least likely to be enjoyed by you, the Robot Smoker.

7. Delay about five minutes between the time you get a desire for each cigarette and the time you actually light it. On occasion, count slowly from one to five before taking the next drag.

8. Don't smoke in one habit area (while you are on the phone, after meals, etc.). Discontinue that particular activity if you decide to smoke. Disconnect these linkages to smoking.

9. Continue to examine your rationalizations.

10. Weigh yourself daily and record it on your weight chart (Appendix 3).

11. Reread the "Exercises" section once each day. This is most important.

Also, wait a full week before you begin the next step, and practice what you learned.

Allies In The War Against The Robot Smoker

This is the third step (week 3) in the plan to slowly free yourself of the smoking habit. If you have made it this far and practiced the exercises in week 2, then you are on your way to quitting.

Note that the act of smoking is connected to far more than just the feeling of smoke filling your lungs and the consequential change in your blood chemistry; all your organs are "tied" to it.

Try the following experiment two or three times this week. Smoke a whole cigarette with your eyes completely closed while you reduce your sense of smell by breathing in and out through your mouth. You probably know already that smoking is not going to be as "pleasurable" under these circumstances, and now you can begin to understand why.

Whether or not you are a chain smoker, it is essential to do an exercise that heightens your awareness of your bodily processes.

Take the time now to remember when you first smoked and inhaled. Virtually 100 percent of all smokers had periods of dizziness, nausea (even vomiting) coughing, headaches, and the like when they started smoking. They were, in fact, made literally sick by smoking. The body reacted violently to the poisons being introduced into the body.

To become a smoker you had to overcome physical resistance and virtually beat your body into submission. After a while, if you do not pay attention to the messages your body sends you, it stops. The Robot Smoker has taken control.

If you had the "willpower" to overcome your body's violent resistance to smoking, you have more than enough to overcome the resistance to quitting.

To support the "self" with helpful and healing procedures is a good way to win the war with the Robot Smoker within you.

Use these techniques to minimize the withdrawal effects of cutting your consumption. You may be surprised if you never experience withdrawal symptoms! In my case, as a heavy smoker, I experienced none!

By this week you will have substantially reduced the number of cigarettes you smoke. You will very likely have a craving for one when you have decided not to yield to the nagging demands of the Robot Smoker.

ADDITIONAL QUIT SMOKING ALLIES

Use these allies as a substitute, a means to get through the craving period, which most often only lasts a short time. Be sure to use all of them at one time or another. Don't limit your allies!

Relaxation breathing: Smoking is pleasurable to some people because it involves the act of rhythmic deep breathing. Deep inhalation and exhalation is for all of us. It is like sighing when we are troubled or anxious—it breaks the tension connected.

Why not use these deep breathing exercises, without the smoke, to help you relax? Try these exercises:

1. Sit in a chair, legs uncrossed, spine straight but relaxed.

2. Take a long deep breath through your nose, mouth closed until your rib cage and chest are fully expanded.

3. Hold your breath for about 10 seconds, and then exhale exclusively through your mouth, all at once, allowing your chest to relax abruptly with a sigh.

4. Let 10 seconds pass, then repeat the breathing pattern. After another 10 seconds do it a third time.

5. Wait about 30 seconds and then repeat the entire cycle of three relaxation breaths. Two or three cycles should produce the desired effects, though one is often sufficient.

Do the relaxation breathing exercise while sitting, because it may make you feel slightly light-headed for a few seconds, a result of the enriched supply of oxygen to your brain.

Notice how much more relaxed you are after this exercise.

RELAXATION AND IMAGERY

This ally will help if you feel jittery or tense as you withdraw from cigarettes (all temporary feelings). Try combining it with relaxation breathing.

In a quiet spot, sit still with your eyes closed and try to picture a favorite idyllic scene, like watching a river flow gently by, or having Sunday morning breakfast in bed with the paper, or lying on a hillside watching white clouds drift against a blue sky.

THE PACIFIER

Oral cravings often increase when we are feeling anxious. Frequently we find ourselves eating more, even though we are not hungry, because occupying our mouths diverts attention from elsewhere and binds nervous energy.

For some people, putting a cigarette in their mouth and drawing on it is much like a baby's pacifier—it calms and comforts.

So why not use a pacifier that is neither harmful nor fattening, expensive or inconvenient and leaves a pleasant scent on your breath. Suck on a clove! That's right, an ordinary clove. Use the best available. They taste better, and you're going to be using quite a few of them in the months to come. Carry a supply from now on. Whenever you desire to not smoke, pop a clove into your mouth.

PHYSICAL EXERCISES

Physical exercise is one of the most important factors in a successful stop-smoking program, but is often entirely overlooked. You can increase your exercise by taking the stairs rather than the elevator, parking the car a block or two from your destination, by getting off the bus one or two stops before or after your destination, or by going for short walks after work. If you prefer you can run in place, do jumping jacks, arm lifts, knee bends, sit-ups, push-ups or any other exercise.

This might also be the time to take up tennis, jumping rope, calisthenics, bicycling, akido or any other sport or activity if you haven't already. But begin modestly. Remember to associate exercise with having fun, so get the right equipment.

BLOCKADING

By using this technique, the "self" builds up a psychological barrier or blockade against the "message" or impulse to smoke until the impulse dies down. Blockading is always available wherever you are or whatever you're doing.

Blockading is a simple mental function in which the voice of your "self" uses a word or phrase as a barrier to drown out the voice of the Robot Smoker, to keep it from "getting through." By rapidly repeating a word or phrase like—No! or Stop!—you will tide your "self" over the brief Robot Smoker attack.

The impulse to smoke will be short-lived, so your use of an ally such as blockading or visualizing can be brief as well.

A MOST IMPORTANT EXERCISE IN THIS PROGRAM: PRINT THE WORDS "THE LAST" IN LARGE LETTERS ON A CIGARETTE IN YOUR CURRENT PACK. DO THIS NOW. DO NOT SMOKE THIS CIGARETTE UNTIL YOU RECEIVE FURTHER INSTRUCTIONS LATER IN THIS PROGRAM. TRANSFER THIS "LAST" CIGARETTE FROM PACK TO PACK THIS WEEK, KEEPING IT WITH YOU AT ALL TIMES.

MORE EXERCISES FOR WEEK THREE

1. Practice daily visualization of burning your last pack of cigarettes.

2. Cut your daily intake of cigarettes by one third.

3. Keep wrapping your cigarette packs in newspaper.

4. Keep using your "Health Bank" for the money you are saving by not smoking as much.

5. Continue to smoke the "anticigarette" brand.

6. Continue using delay periods before each cigarette and occasionally before taking the next drag.

7. Don't smoke in the "knee jerk" area you selected previously. Select a new area this week and don't smoke there either.

8. Continue to examine your rationalizations. Write them down. Think about the "loopholes" in them.

9. Two or three times this week light and smoke a whole cigarette with your eyes closed while breathing through your mouth. Pay attention to how much less "pleasurable" it is.

10. Two times this week, sit down, face a blank wall and in a rapid fashion smoke two cigarettes one directly after the other. Pay careful attention to changes in your bodily processes as you do so.

11. Continue to weigh yourself daily.

12. Use the "allies" as liberally and often as possible. Where necessary, reread the descriptions: relaxation breathing, relaxation imagery, the pacifiers (especially whole cloves), physical exercise (start small, go slowly, have fun, keep up your momentum), blockading (with and without visualization) and other allies you have adapted on your own.

13. Mark the "The Last" cigarette. Don't smoke it but transfer it from pack to pack.

14. If you have extra packs of cigarettes use them up. Buy only one pack at a time this week.

15. Reread the "Pitfalls" and the "Exercises" section once each day).

Wait exactly one week before you begin the next phase and practice what you learned.

The Critical Week

SMOKING THAT FINAL CIGARETTE WON'T BE VERY PLEASANT, BUT IT WILL BE VERY MEMORABLE!!!!!!!!!

After battling to the very doors of the non-smokers club, many cigarette users are swept away in a rush or last minute deceptions that leave them firmly hooked as ever. This is the fourth step of a week-by-week plan. This should be clipped and saved so each step of the plan can be fulfilled.

In your pack of cigarettes is "The Last" one you will ever smoke. You've been transferring it from pack to pack this past week. If you have been thinking that you are going to smoke "The Last" in a positive, pleasant way, now's the time to learn why that idea is the exact opposite of what should be the case.

Go before the bathroom mirror with your current cigarette pack, matches and some cloves.

Take "The Last" cigarette and rewrap the pack as usual. You are about to smoke "The Last" cigarette of your life in a deliberately counter-hypnotic way so that your last memory will be an ally to your "self," not an ally to the Robot Smoker.

Look at the words "The Last" printed on the cigarette and repeat them to yourself a few times. Consider what this means—the very last cigarette you will ever smoke! Do this slowly, seriously with concentration and full awareness: think deeply and calmly. Keep checking to make sure that your attention is sharp and focused on what you are saying. The Robot Smoker may try to dull or divert your attention in some way.

Face a mirror and put "The Last" cigarettes in your lips so that the words on it are visible in the mirror, and drop your remaining cigarettes (whether it has 0 or 19 left in it) into the empty sink.

Next, light "The Last" cigarette and with the same match light the pack of cigarettes in the sink. Get a really good blaze going on the pack of cigarettes, using as many matches as you need.

Then puff on the "The Last" cigarette as fast as you can, inhaling as usual, while looking in the mirror and watching the last cigarette going up in smoke, dissolve in ashes. Try to visualize and see in your mind's eye the image you have previously visualized during the course of this program, the one in which you tossed your last package of cigarettes into a blazing fire. Try to superimpose this image upon the burning pack.

NOTE:

The ritual of burning the "The Last" might also be done outside (with or without mirrors) on your patio, etc. with your family or close friends in attendance. Make this a big, exciting and memorable moment!

And when you have puffed away on the "The Last" cigarette, wash your hands and face, gargle and wash out your mouth with some cool water or mouthwash, and then brush your teeth.

It is quite likely that years of practice in bringing your hand up to your mouth, with a cigarette in it have caused you to develop a powerful association between that hand and smoking. The following technique will help remind you not to smoke when you glance at your hand. Do this now and repeat it each morning for at least the next month or two before you start your day.

In letters about ½ inch high, print "I.Q." on the front of the lower joint of the thumb on the hand you used to smoke with. Use a ballpoint pen or fine-pointed marking pen and replace the letters during the day if you happen to wash them off.

The "I.Q." should be obvious.

SUMMARY: BREAKING A HABIT/RATIONALIZATIONS

1. "What the hell." In this ruse the Robot Smoker tells the "self" that, "Since the air is polluted by the industrial wastes…" or, "Since I could develop a disease because of atomic testing or chemicals in my food stopping smoking is irrelevant." Of course, death is an inevitability for all of us, but that doesn't suggest we should do anything to bring it on sooner or increase our chances of falling ill. The healthy "self" wants to preserve life and enhance wellbeing. This ruse is obviously and ridiculously nonsensical.

2. "This is killing me." There is no temporary discomfort that will "kill" you as surely as cigarettes will. This is killing me" is nonsense based on a total reversal of the truth.

3. "I've got it licked." Remember the old saying, "Pride goeth before the fall." This ruse is used usually by the Robot Smoker at times when you have not wanted to smoke for a while and have not been lulled into a false security.

    The rationalization is: "I'm only going to smoke one cigarette (or however many), or take one drag (or more), just to show that it doesn't affect me, or how I completely kicked the habit, or how I can put cigarettes away any time I want (etc. etc., etc.)." Ask yourself just what purpose would be served by engaging in experiments proposed by the Robot Smoker.

    If you care to demonstrate your "willpower," do it in a sane, healthy way: choose not to smoke no matter what the Robot Smoker suggests. And beware of letting yourself become smug or complacent about your progress.

4. "I didn't want to quit anyway." Based on the crudest denial of truth, this ruse tries to suggest that "I only wanted to prove myself that I could stop anytime I wanted to. Now that I stopped (for days, weeks, months), I'll start again and stop permanently when I really want." You can recognize a variation of this ruse in the old comic saying: "Stopping smoking is easy—I've done it dozens of times."

Again, welcome to the ranks of nonsmokers. Have a clove, go for a walk, lie in the sun, get an ice cream cone, take a hot bath, or do all of the above—or do something that your "self" enjoys. Hang in there. For a good many of you, the hardest moments have already occurred.

AFTER-QUITTING EXERCISES

Congratulations—you have licked the Robot Smoker and you are now free of smoking. It is recommended that you continue to perform the exercises below:

1. Continue to save money in the "Health Bank" for each cigarette you are now not smoking.

2. Continue to examine your rationalizations. Continue to write them down.

3. Weigh yourself daily or, if you prefer, somewhat less often and chart it as you have been doing.

4. Use all the "Allies" as liberally as possible. Keep cloves or other allies with you at all times.

5. Continue doing your daily physical exercises. If possible, increase them slightly.

6. Put the letters "I.Q." on the thumb of the hand you used to smoke with. Renew the letters as they wear off. They should be clear and present from the time you arise until the time you go to bed. Do this every day.

7. Throw out all cigarettes and butts wherever you find them. Put away all the paraphernalia of cigarettes: ashtrays, lighters, cigarettes cases, etc.

8. Be an ally to your "self" and watch your health gradually improve. If you should feel in need of help reread this material and practice what you've learned.

Post Smoking

HOW TO CONTINUE TO KEEP FROM STARTING SMOKING AGAIN, AND WAYS TO OVERCOME THE URGE TO LIGHT UP ANOTHER CIGARETTE

After quitting for weeks, the urge may return for some smokers. Here are some techniques for resisting the nagging desires to smoke, and situations that make it harder to abstain.

Each additional week that you don't smoke increases the likelihood that you will become a lifelong nonsmoker.

THE MOST DIFFICULT PERIOD FOR MOST PEOPLE AS YOU MAY HAVE SUPPOSED, IS DURING THE FIRST WEEKS OF ABSTINENCE!

But if you happen to be among those who the intense pressure to smoke does not let up rather substantially by the end of the first or second week, don't despair—you are not alone.

Whenever you feel impatient or anxious or a bit disheartened, ask yourself, "What ally can I use to make me feel better?" Above all DO NOT be passive in the face of any unpleasant feeling connected to smoking; YOU MUST ACT! You must help the "self" to the help that is available.

THE SPOILER TECHNIQUE

Help can include a new technique for this program. It depends on the delivery of an unpleasant stimulus to the Robot Smoker for its effect. I call the technique "The Spoiler," because it spoils the attempts of the Robot Smoker to retain or regain control over the "self."

Get a rubber band (one about 1/8" is ideally suitable for this purpose) that will fit comfortably—not too tightly or too loosely—around your wrists from day to day. Whenever you get the urge, snap the band around your wrist by stretching it several inches and then letting go. Alternate snapping it against either sides of the inner or outer part your wrists. Keep snapping it until the desire to smoke abates for at least 15 seconds.

The Robot Smoker is learning that every time he pressures you it is going to get painfully punished until it stops. Soon it will send messages much less frequently, and when the messages do appear they will be much weaker.

In order for the Spoiler to work, however, you must be sure that the snap of the rubber band:

1. Causes pain but doesn't cut your skin or damage you in any way.

2. Is delivered as soon as the nagging begins.

3. Continues until the urge leaves for at least 15 seconds.

Plan to use The Spoiler consistently for a month or more. It should be worn around your wrist from the moment you get up until the moment you retire. It's a good idea to keep a spare rubber band with you in case yours breaks. Don't be caught unprepared.

Rare occasions may arise when someone will try to undermine you, usually by making fun of your techniques or by taunting you "good-naturedly" by purposely blowing smoke in your direction or insistently "pushing" a cigarette at you.

These maneuvers are gallows humor, situations which are something that is essentially very serious and potentially damaging is cloaked in jest.

There's no reason to get heavy-handed or angry with such persons, but don't cooperate or collude with them. Don't smile back at them. At the least, look in their eyes with an impassive "flat" expression that says, "I don't like your message and I'm not going to pretend that I do."

An even better response, however, is more active. In a pleasant but serious manner you might say, "Please don't do that. I really am quitting smoking, and what you just did makes it harder for me to quit smoking."

This way of relating can even transform underminers into allies, perhaps to the point where they might be stimulated to begin a stop-smoking program themselves. Fellow "stoppers" often make the best allies.

There will be moments when you get pressure from the Robot Smoker, but not smoking will most certainly become more and more natural as time passes.

Be patient and keep working. Soon you will notice how much easier it has become not to smoke, or has that day already occurred?

In the event you get pressure from the Robot Smoker and have a sudden urge to smoke, there is a great deal you can do to get rid of it. Here are some possibilities:

1. Analyze its source. Why did the urge occur? What or who triggered it? What associations were activated? Were you feeling angry or frustrated because of something that happened or didn't happen? Were you really just bored? Did someone near you light up, or someone in the film you saw?

2. What ruse is accompanying it? What rationalization is your Robot Smoker suggesting that you use?

3. What do you want that a cigarette is a substitute for? Were you really hungry or thirsty or tired instead? What healthy way can you find to comfort or support your "self?" What harmless substitutes can you make use of (remember the cloves)? If you can't get what you like at the moment, either do without it or delay doing anything about it until it is possible to get.

4. What allies can you make use of? Use the Spoiler. Use as many allies as you need. Do something else, somewhere else.

Above all, remember that time is definitely on your side in this project of self-improvement. If and when an urge comes upon you, by now even a simple decision is very much weaker than it was and growing more so every day—and the power of your healthy "self" is increasing.

ADDITIONAL POST SMOKING EXERCISES

1. Use the Spoiler for the next two weeks, after which you are to change your technique as follows:

    Starting two weeks from now, instead of snapping the rubber band against your wrist every time you feel the urge to smoke, snap it only every other time. If and when the urges arise, deal with them in other ways: use diversions, substitutes, anything that works.

    After two weeks at this 50 percent level, begin to snap the rubber band on a random or intermittent fashion.

    Continue to wear the rubber band until a month has passed without you having had any strong impulses to smoke.

    Return to using the Spoiler any time in the future that you feel the need for some quick and effective help. During these times, use it just as you did during the first two weeks.

2. Continue to inscribe "I.Q." on your thumb for at least one more month.

3. Continue doing your daily physical exercise.

And now that you made it this far, GOOD LUCK—YOU ARE NOW A NON-SMOKER!

NOTES:

If you should stumble at the first attempt in following the program, don't give up but try starting again. You may find that since you now know the gist of the program and the pitfall(s), you might retry following the program again—and be successful!

You may know someone, a relative or friend who also is contemplating to quit smoking. This might be a great time for the two of you to become "allies" in your quest to quit and provide immeasurable support to each other.

APPENDIX 1

Rationalizations

Mark an "X" adjacent to the column for the specific realizations that might pertain to you at times during this program.

RATIONALIZATION	PERTAINS TO ME						
I don't smoke enough to harm myself							
Oh...what the hell....if it's not one thing it's another							
Cigarettes relax me							
Cigarettes "pep" me up							
I'll gain too much weight							
I don't have the will power							

Tracking Daily Weight During Program

Weigh yourself each day during the program and track your progress, you might find that weight gain was not an issue.

DAYS	WEEK 1	WEEK 2	WEEK 3	WEEK 4	WEEK 5	WEEK 6	WEEK 7
1							
2							
3							
4							
5							
6							
7							

APPENDIX 3

Breathing & Imaging Chart

Mark an "X" each time you perform the breathing exercises and develop a clear image of burning your "Last Cigarette" in a blazing fire.

DAYS	5 MINUTE PERIODS						
WEEK 1	1	2	3	4	5	6	7
1							
2							
3							
4							
5							
6							
7							

WEEK 2						
1						
2						
3						
4						
5						
6						
7						

WEEK 3						
1						
2						
3						
4						
5						
6						
7						

WEEK 4						
1						
2						
3						
4						
5						
6						
7						

APPENDIX 4

Exercise Monitoring

For each of the exercises you choose to follow, record the duration of each that you do daily.

EXERCISE 1 ___________________________

WEEK	MONDAY	TUESDAY	WEDNESDAY	THURSDAY	FRIDAY	SATURDAY	SUNDAY
1							
2							
3							
4							

EXERCISE 2 ____________________________

WEEK	MONDAY	TUESDAY	WEDNESDAY	THURSDAY	FRIDAY	SATURDAY	SUNDAY
1							
2							
3							
4							

Tracking Daily Cigarette Consumption

The goal here is to reduce the number of cigarettes you smoke each week by one-third.

Count the number of cigarettes you smoked each day for the first week. Add the daily figures and divide by seven to get a daily average. Divide this average by three and subtract this number from the daily average of the first week to get the number of cigarettes you will smoke each day during the second week, etc. for the third week.

NUMBER CIGARETTES CONSUMED EACH DAY			
DAY	WEEK 1	WEEK 2	WEEK 3
1			
2			
3			
4			
5			
6			
7			
TOTAL			
AVERAGE/DAY DIVIDE BY 7			
DIVIDE ABOVE AVERAGE BY 3			

Examples:

WEEK 2:

Say you smoke 126 cigarettes.

1. Add the daily number of cigarettes you smoke per week (126)
2. Divide this number by 7 (126/7) to get a daily average (18).
3. Divide the daily average by 3 (18/3) =6.
4. Subtract 6 from daily average (18-6=12).
5. This is the number of cigarettes (12) you will smoke each day in Week 2.

WEEK 3:

1. Divide the second week daily average by 7 (i.e. daily average=12)
2. Divide this daily by 3 (12/3=4)
3. Subtract this number from the daily average of week 2 (12-4=8).
4. This is the number of cigarettes you will smoke in Week 3.

APPENDIX 6

Personal Conditioned Reflexes

Place a check after each reflex or habit that encourages you to light up.
There may be others not listed in this chart. If so, add them below.

CONDITIONED REFLEXES	
With coffee	
After a meal	
While watching TV	
While having a drink	
Smoking after sex	
Before bedtime	
Other #1	
Other #2	